Made in the USA
Middletown, DE
31 May 2020

96393575R00066